The Big Clock!
A Kid's Guide To Munich, Germany

Photography By John D. Weigand
Poetry By Penelope Dyan

Bellissima Publishing, LLC
Jamul, California
www.bellissimapublishing.com

Copyright © 2013 by Penny D. Weigand and John D. Weigand

All rights reserved. No part of this book may be
reproduced or transmitted in any form or by any means,
electronic or mechanical, including photocopying,
recording, or by any other means, or by any information or
storage retrieval system, without permission from the publisher.

ISBN 978-1-61477-080-0
First Edition

"Pick my left pocket of its silver dime, but spare the right – it holds my golden time!"

OLIVER WENDELL HOLMES

The Big Clock!
Bellissima Publishing, LLC

Introduction

Munich is the capital and the largest city of the German state of Bavaria and is located on the River Isar, north of the Bavarian Alps. It is the third largest city in Germany, right behind the cities of Berlin and Hamburg. And while all of this may be very interesting to an adult, tell this to a child and that child will yawn and think, "Boy, is that boring!"

There are no such boring facts in this book written by the award winning author, attorney and former teacher, Penelope Dyan and complemented with the photographs of John D. Weigand, former television director of engineering. This book is strictly for kids and shows the things that really catch the eyes of a child.

Mixed into this is a text that uses word recognition and rhyme so that a kid can shout out what is coming next and thereby enhance reading skills! Then to make the learning process even more fun, look for the music video that goes along with this book. You can find it on the Bellissimavideo Channel on YouTube. The Dyan/Weigand books are about imparting the love and joy of learning to a kid, and nothing more, proving once again you simply can't go wrong with a Bellissima Book!

The Big Clocky!
Bellissima Publishing, LLC

The Big Clock!
A Kid's Guide To Munich, Germany

Photography By John D. Weigand
Poetry By Penelope Dyan

You're in Munich, Germany!
The architecture is beyond compare,
And so you stop and you really stare.
Your mom and dad tell you quite a lot,
but you're really only interested
in that famous old clock.

And then you see it!
It's the Glockenspiel, after all.
And it's just sitting there on that wall!
You hope that if you get a chance,
you'll be there when the figurines dance!

There is an elegant looking building and loads of shops.
Over here Mom will make several stops!

You see an beautiful ornate arch,
so what do you do?
You walk right to it
AND you go right through!

It is beautiful inside
and there is a statue of gold
that you decide is VERY old.

And then right out of that door you go,
as your mom and dad remind you
to NOT walk so slow.
After all, you MUST get on your way,
because, you see, it's a very BIG day.

You see a church
and you see a steeple,
and in the streets
you see some people.

It is nearing Christmas
and a Santa plays
a musical number or two.
You stop and drop a coin
in his accordion case,
and then he smiles at you.

Next you examine the paw of a lion,
and you tell him to have a good day.
Then you bid him a fond
"Auf Wiedersehen,"
as you skip merrily away.

Here is a place that is a very good find,
if like mom and dad,
you have strudel and coffee
on your mind.
And as to the strudel you really do!
And so you all stop for a bite or two!

Then you see on a table of red,
the Chistmas geese,
each one has no head.
You think that here in Munich
(if you were a goose)
that it would NOT be good
to be caught out on the loose.
Or you might end up as someone's feast,
sitting there on the table
with the pie and roast beast!

You go back to where the clock was,
right there at the start.
You decide Munich is a fun place
with lots of music
and with your kind of art.
After all, you have seen a cool lion,
and walked through a castle-like door,
you've eaten some really great strudel,
and your mom says there's even more!
And tonight when you go to bed
visions of Bratwurst
will dance through your head!

"When the music changes, so does the dance."

AFRICAN PROVERB

www.ingramcontent.com/pod-product-compliance
Ingram Content Group UK Ltd.
Pitfield, Milton Keynes, MK11 3LW, UK
UKHW060135240426
12048UKWH00002B/41